Lerner SPORTS

SPORTS TEAM SMACKDOWN

US WOMEN'S HOCKEY VS. CANADA WOMEN'S HOCKEY

BATTLE FOR OLYMPIC GOLD

JASON M. BURNS

Lerner Publications ◆ Minneapolis

To all young athletes and dreamers. Practice doesn't make perfect, it makes progress. Be the best you there is, not the best that ever was.

The stats and information in this book are accurate through the 2026 Winter Olympics.

Lerner Publications Company
An imprint of Lerner Publishing Group, Inc.
241 First Avenue North
Minneapolis, MN 55401 USA

For reading levels and more information, look up this title at www.lernerbooks.com.

Main body text set in Aptifer Sans LT Pro.
Typeface provided by Linotype AG.

Library of Congress Cataloging-in-Publication Data

The Cataloging-in-Publication Data for *US Women's Hockey vs. Canada Women's Hockey: Battle for Olympic Gold* is on file at the Library of Congress.

ISBN 979-8-3480-6908-7 (lib. bdg.)
ISBN 979-8-3480-6915-5 (pbk)
ISBN 979-8-3480-6919-3 (epub)

Manufactured in the United States of America
1 – 7/15/26

TABLE OF CONTENTS

INTRODUCTION

NEXT-DOOR NEIGHBORS

The Team USA Hockey women's team and the Canada National Women's Hockey Team have one of the greatest rivalries in sports. They have squared off in the biggest games in ice hockey for more than 30 years. The two teams were playing in the gold medal game of the 2026 Winter Olympics in Milan, Italy, on February 19, 2026. Team USA had already beaten Team Canada 5–0 earlier in the tournament. But Team Canada was there to win.

Team USA's Joy Dunne (center) and Claire Thompson (left) of Team Canada fight for the puck during the 2026 Olympics.

Both teams were having trouble scoring. The game was tied 1–1 at the end of regulation time. But in overtime, US forward Taylor Heise passed the puck down the ice to Megan Keller. Keller rushed toward Team Canada's goal. She slapped the puck past the goalie to score and win the game. Team USA had won their third gold medal. They were undefeated in the tournament, giving up only two goals in seven games.

FAST FACTS

- Team USA won the first-ever Olympic gold medal in women's hockey.
- Team USA was undefeated in the 2026 Olympics. They had five straight shutouts, which is an Olympic record.
- Team Canada has won five Olympic gold medals in women's hockey.
- Canada held the first international women's hockey tournament in 1987.

Team Canada has also had its share of overtime magic. They won Olympic gold in 2002, 2006, and 2010. They wanted to make it four in a row at the 2014 Winter Olympics in Sochi, Russia. Team Canada just had to beat Team USA to win gold.

Team USA dominated most of the game. Team Canada was down 2–0 with only four minutes left in regulation time. Any hope of winning gold was slipping away. But then something incredible happened.

Team Canada scored two goals to tie the game. Marie-Philip Poulin scored one of them. She is one of the most successful women's hockey players of all time. Poulin scored again in overtime, leading Team Canada to its fourth gold medal in a row.

Team USA and Team Canada have won more big games than any other national teams in the sport. But which one is best? Let the smackdown begin!

Team USA's Jocelyne Lamoureux-Davidson (left) battles Team Canada's Hayley Irwin (right) during the gold medal game of the 2014 Olympics.

SMACKDOWN!

CHAPTER 1

Members of Team Canada celebrate their ninth World Championship win over Team USA in 2007.

RIVALRY REPEATED

The United States women's national hockey team started in 1987. They played their first game on April 21, 1987, against Canada. Canada won 2–1, setting the stage for a long and heated rivalry between the two teams.

Canada held the first women's international ice hockey tournament in 1987. But Team Canada did not officially start until 1990. It formed that year to compete in the first Women's World Championship. Team Canada won the tournament, defeating Team USA 5–2 in the final game.

Team USA celebrates winning the first-ever gold medal for women's hockey at the 1998 Olympics.

Team USA and Team Canada often meet in big games. Either Team USA or Team Canada has won every women's hockey Olympic gold medal and every Women's World Championship. The teams are made up of some of the best players in the world. Many of them are teammates in the Professional Women's Hockey League (PWHL). Playing against—and with—one another keeps the rivalry going.

Team Canada's Sarah Nurse (center) controls the puck at the 2026 Olympics in a match against Team USA.

Canada and the United States are the only two teams to win gold for women's hockey at the Winter Olympics.

The Winter Olympics is international hockey's biggest stage. Team USA struck first in the rivalry with Canada, winning the first Olympic gold medal in women's ice hockey in 1998. Team Canada won the next four. Team Canada leads Team USA in Olympic gold medal wins 5–3.

CHECK IT OUT

The 1998 Winter Olympics took place in Nagano, Japan.

Team Canada players hold flowers and gold medals during the medal ceremony at the 2014 Olympics.

Team USA players line up for the gold medal match against Canada at the 1998 Olympics. It was the first time women's hockey was played at the Olympic Games.

The Women's World Championship started in 1990. Team Canada has won the tournament 13 times. Team USA has won it 11 times. No other team in the world has ever won the World Championship, but Finland has the most third-place finishes.

No matter how many times Team USA and Team Canada meet on the ice, the action is always exciting. The athletes take the rivalry as seriously as the fans do. Each team wants to win every time they face off. Only a handful of Team USA and Team Canada's losses have been to other teams. Canada currently leads the United States in head-to-head matchups 106–88.

CHAPTER 2

US goalie Sarah Tueting (top left) and two Team USA defenders fight to block a shot from Team Canada during the 1998 Olympics.

AMAZING MOMENTS

In 1998, Team USA met Team Canada in the first Olympic final on February 17. The game was scoreless in the first period. But then Team USA took control. They were ahead 2–1 with only seconds left in the third period.

Team Canada was desperate. As time ran out, they pulled their goalie from the game and put in a player who could score. But the move didn't work. Sandra Whyte of Team USA took advantage and scored an empty-net goal. Team USA won the gold 3–1. They were undefeated in the Olympics and outscored their opponents 36–8.

Twenty years later, at the 2018 Winter Olympics, Team USA was facing Team Canada in the final game again. Team Canada had defeated Team USA in the gold medal match at the 2002, 2010, and 2014 Olympics. This time, the results would be different.

Kendall Coyne (left) and Hilary Knight (right) circle the ice with the United States flag after their victory over Canada at the 2018 Olympics.

Jocelyne Lamoureux-Davidson (right) *tries to score during the shoot-out at the 2018 gold medal game.*

Monique Lamoureux-Morando scored a goal for Team USA late in regulation time to force overtime. After neither team scored in overtime, the game moved to a shoot-out. Jocelyne Lamoureux-Davidson scored in the sixth round of the shoot-out, winning the gold for Team USA. It was their first gold medal in 20 years.

In 2026, Team USA dominated throughout the Olympics. They outscored their opponents 33–2 and set an Olympic record for most shutouts in a row, with five. In the first round on February 10, 2026, Team USA beat Team Canada 5–0. It was Team Canada's first Olympic shutout loss.

Team Canada was unstoppable in the first Women's World Championship in 1990. Wearing pink-and-white jerseys, the team went undefeated throughout the tournament. They were down by two goals early in the final game against Team USA before coming back to finish strong. Team Canada defeated Team USA 5–2 to win gold. The tournament set Team Canada up as the dominant force in women's ice hockey for the next 20 years.

Team Canada's Jayna Hefford (center) celebrates a goal against Team USA at the 2002 Olympics.

Members of Team Canada celebrate their fifth Olympic gold medal in 2022.

Canada fans were disappointed when the national team lost the first Olympic gold medal to Team USA. They were out for revenge when they met the United States again in the final game of the 2002 Winter Olympics in Salt Lake City, Utah. The game was extremely tough and hard-fought, but Team Canada defeated Team USA 3–2. The victory gave Canada its first gold medal in Olympic women's hockey.

CHECK IT OUT

Team USA's Monique Lamoureux-Morando and Jocelyne Lamoureux-Davidson are identical twin sisters. As teammates, they have won two Olympic silver medals and one gold medal.

Winning became common for Team Canada over the next few decades. They won four Olympic gold medals in a row from 2002 to 2014. Team Canada won their fifth gold on February 17, 2022. Canadian hockey hero Marie-Philip Poulin confirmed her status as an all-time great player by scoring twice against Team USA in the final game. She led Canada to a 3–2 victory.

Monique Lamoureux-Morando (left) and Jocelyne Lamoureux-Davidson (right) joined the US Hockey Hall of Fame in 2022.

CHAPTER 3

Team USA's Hilary Knight is the all-time leader in goals, assists, and points at the Women's World Championship.

TOP PLAYERS

US forward Hilary Knight is one of the best players in the sport. She is a five-time Olympian and has competed in 10 World Championships. Knight holds the record for most Olympic goals for Team USA with 15. She won gold medals in 2018 and 2026.

Angela Ruggiero helped bring attention to women's ice hockey in the United States. She holds the record for most games played for Team USA by a man or woman with

256. She is a four-time Olympian and has won 10 World Championships. Ruggiero also became the first woman who didn't play goalie to compete in a pro men's hockey league when she played for the Central Hockey League in 2005.

In 2015, Angela Ruggiero of Team USA became only the fourth woman and second American woman to join the Hockey Hall of Fame.

Amanda Kessel scored 50 goals in 126 games with Team USA.

Amanda Kessel was already a hockey superstar before she joined Team USA. She won three college championships with the University of Minnesota. Kessel is a three-time Olympian and played in seven World Championships. Her shoot-out goal at the 2018 Olympics helped give Team USA its first gold medal in 20 years.

Known by her nickname Captain Clutch, Marie-Philip Poulin is one of the most successful ice hockey players of all time. She has won three Olympic gold medals with Team Canada and scored the game-winning goals in each victory. Poulin holds the record for most all-time Olympic goals with 20. She is the captain of the Montreal Victoire in the PWHL.

Marie-Philip Poulin is the only hockey player to score in four Olympic gold medal games in a row.

Many fans consider Hayley Wickenheiser to be the greatest female hockey player in the history of the sport. She won four Olympic gold medals and seven World Championships. She retired in 2017 as Team Canada's all-time leader in goals with 168 and assists with 211. Wickenheiser also represented Team Canada in softball at the 2000 Summer Olympics. She became a doctor after retiring from ice hockey.

In 2002–2003, Hayley Wickenheiser played on a men's team in Finland.

Sarah Fillier was the first player in PWHL history to score in five games in a row. In 2025, she became a captain of her team, the New York Sirens.

Sarah Fillier is part of a new group of great Canadian hockey players. She was selected first overall in the 2024 PWHL Draft. The league named her Rookie of the Year after her first season. Fillier won an Olympic gold medal with Team Canada in 2022, scoring eight goals, the second-highest total on the team.

CHECK IT OUT

The PWHL launched in 2024. It expanded from six to eight teams for the 2025–2026 season.

CHAPTER 4

Team Canada has won gold or silver in every Olympics since 1998.

CHOOSE YOUR CHAMPION

Team USA and Team Canada are two of the best women's ice hockey teams in the world, but which one comes out on top? There's no right or wrong answer. Different people will have different opinions.

Team USA has reached the gold-medal game in every Women's World Championship tournament since it started in 1990. They have won it 11 times. They have also won three gold and four silver medals at the Winter Olympics. Team

Canada has won five gold and three silver Olympic medals. They have also won 13 Women's World Championships.

Team USA and Team Canada have either been the best or the second-best in the world for many years. No other country has come close to their greatness. And the PWHL has only strengthened the rivalry.

Team Canada leads slightly in head-to-head matchups, but Team USA has been dominant in the 2020s. Team USA's dramatic victories—along with the country's growing women's ice hockey culture—puts them ahead of Team Canada just enough to win this smackdown.

What do you think? Did we get it right? Think about why or why not!

Fifteen of Team USA's 23 players scored during the 2026 Olympics. Many consider the team to be the best US women's hockey team of all time.

SMACKDOWN TIMELINE

WOMEN'S TEAM USA HOCKEY

1987 Women's Team USA Hockey is formed.

1990 The team plays in its first major tournament, the Women's World Championship.

1998 Team USA wins the first-ever Olympic gold medal in women's ice hockey.

2005 After a shoot-out, Team USA wins its first Women's World Championship gold medal.

2008 Team USA wins the first of three Women's World Championships in a row.

2013 Team USA wins the first of six Women's World Championships in a row.

2018 The team wins its second Olympic gold medal.

2026 Megan Keller scores a goal in overtime to give Team USA its third Olympic gold medal.

WOMEN'S TEAM CANADA HOCKEY

1987 Canada plays in its first international game, defeating Switzerland 10–0.

1990 The Canada National Women's Hockey Team is formed.

1990 Team Canada wins the first-ever Women's World Championship gold medal.

2002 After losing to Team USA in 1998, Team Canada wins their first Olympic gold medal. They win gold in the next three Winter Olympics.

2017 Hayley Wickenheiser retires from hockey.

2021 Team Canada wins the first of two Women's World Championships in a row.

2022 The team wins its fifth Olympic gold medal.

2024 The PWHL establishes pro teams in Canadian cities Toronto, Ottawa, and Montreal.

2026 Team Canada falls to Team USA in the Olympic gold medal game.

GLOSSARY

draft: when teams take turns choosing new players

forward: a player whose main job is to score goals

overtime: an extra period played to determine a winner when the score is tied

period: one of three 20-minute sections of a hockey game

regulation time: the standard length of a game, not including overtime

rivalry: when two teams compete against each other over a long period of time

rookie: a first-year player

shoot-out: a shooting contest in overtime that is used to determine the winner of a game tied at the end of regulation time

shutout: when a team plays an entire game and does not allow a goal to be scored against them

tournament: a series of games played to determine a champion

LEARN MORE

Burns, Jason M. *US Men's Hockey vs. Canada Men's Hockey: Battle for Olympic Gold*. Lerner Publications, 2027.

Hayley Wickenheiser, Hockey Canada
https://www.hockeycanada.ca/en-ca/exclusive/world-hockey-summit/home/attendees/speakers/hayley-wickenheiser

Hill, Anne E. *Women's Professional Hockey*. Lerner Publications, 2026.

History of Women's Ice Hockey in the United States Facts for Kids
https://kids.kiddle.co/History_of_women%27s_ice_hockey_in_the_United_States

Streeter, Anthony. *Winter Olympics All-Time Greats*. Press Box Books, 2025.

U.S. Women's Olympic History & Records
https://teamusa.usahockey.com/page/show/2906622-u-s-women-s-olympic-history-and-records

INDEX

PHOTO ACKNOWLEDGMENTS

Image credits: Xavier Lane/Getty Images, p. 4; Harry How/Getty Images, p. 7; Elsa/Getty Images, p. 7; Alexander NEMENOV/AFP via Getty Images, p. 8; Bruce Bennett Studios via Getty Images Studios/Getty Images, p. 9; JULIEN DE ROSA/AFP via Getty Images, p. 10; ANTHONY WALLACE/AFP via Getty Images/Getty Images, p. 11; Doug Pensinger/Getty Images, p. 12; David Madison/Getty Images, p. 13; ROBERT SULLIVAN/AFP via Getty Images/Getty Images, p. 14; Harry How/Getty Images, p. 15; Bruce Bennett/Getty Images, p. 16; David Madison/Getty Images, p. 17; Mao Jianjun/China News Service via Getty Images/Getty Images, p. 18; Mike Ehrmann/Getty Images, p. 19; Bruce Bennett/Getty Images, p. 20; Harry How/Getty Images, p. 21; Harry How/Getty Images, p. 22; Elsa/Getty Images, p. 23; Doug Pensinger/Getty Images, p. 24; RvS.Media/Monika Maher/Getty Images, p. 25; Bruce Bennett/Getty Images, p. 26; Sarah Stier/Getty Images, p. 27.

Cover: AP Photo/Hassan Ammar; AP Photo/Carolyn Kaster.